POWER vs. *Heart*

in Leadership

The **FIVE** most important *human* attributes you need
to earn the respect, loyalty and trust of your team

Ovsan

POWER vs. *Heart* in Leadership

For more information visit www.powervsheart.com

Cover design by *Mgo Talarian*

Printed in the United States of America.

PAROV Press

ISBN-13: 978-0615982311
ISBN-10: 061598231X

DEDICATION

In loving memory of my father

Haig Paroyian

I dedicate this book to you, dad, for encouraging me, at a very young age, to read and appreciate a good book. You have instilled in me the love of knowledge and learning. I am forever grateful to you.

May you rest in peace and let light shine upon your beautiful soul.

You are always in my heart!

CONTENTS

CHAPTER II:
The HEART of the matter

CHAPTER III:
Who, What, When, and Why?

CHAPTER IV:
Your True Self

POWER vs. *Heart* in Leadership

ACKNOWLEDGEMENTS

I would like to thank my friends and family who supported me while I worked on my manuscript. I could not have done this without you all.

My appreciation to Murphy Daley, Roberto Ball, Rose Mahouski, and Gerrie for being my beta readers.

My thanks to Bruce Burke for being my sounding board throughout the process.

My special gratitude to Edward Apelian for his detailed and thoughtful feedback.

My love to my sons Mgo and Haig for their patience and willingness to listen as I shared my stories and asked for their input.

My love to my mother, Irma, for keeping me on the right track throughout this journey.

Thank you for helping me make this book possible and achieve a lifelong dream.

INTRODUCTION

Leaders come in all shapes and forms, as do human beings. Some are kind and understanding, some are rude, and others outright egotistical and self-centered.

Leaders who reach a certain rank or position tend to take advantage of the power that comes with the position, throwing their weight around. This gives them the illusion that they are important and mighty. But, do these leaders realize the importance of bringing their hearts along for the ride?

If you come across a leader who treats you as his or her peer and respects you as a human being, listens to your suggestions, and understands where you are coming from, hang on to that leader for dear life—good leaders seem to be scarce in the workplace today.

Throughout my working career, I've had the opportunity to interact with a variety of leaders. It's interesting to note that the years I spent working with leaders who were kind and understanding went by swimmingly fast. I had fun as I learned and grew, not only in my position, but as a human being as well. It's the years I had to spend with the rude and know-it-all leaders that dragged on and almost broke me down, tempting me to just drop everything and walk out—if only it weren't for the paycheck that kept me going! But, most days, I literally had to force myself to get out of bed and drag myself to work. I bet most of you know exactly what I mean.

This book, "**POWER** vs. *Heart* in Leadership," is not intended to be educational or instructional. It doesn't come with any studies or survey results. Instead, it is meant to inspire and touch the hearts of leaders—those just starting their careers and those who have been doing this for a while—with the hope that they can discover their True Selves and, in turn, elevate their teams by encouraging and motivating them.

This book is merely a presentation of my candid observations and personal experiences as an employee, a fellow colleague, and as a leader, of what generally goes on in the workplace.

Over the years, I have done a lot of soul searching, asking myself what it means to be a good human being and how that relates to being a solid leader. I have come to learn that, to be a true leader you have to start with yourself, examining how you can be a good human being first. When you focus on leading with your heart, and not on the power that comes with your position, everything else falls into place naturally.

It's very easy, and, at times tempting, to get swept away by the power that comes with a leadership role. You ask and you receive. People fear your position and always want to please you because you have the power to get them in trouble or even fire them. But, is this the effect you really want to have on others? It's essential to set aside the power that comes with the position, park your ego at the door, and focus on how you can lead with compassion, treating people with respect and dignity. To be an effective leader, it's necessary to first have self-awareness and focus within.

As you read this book, keep an open mind. If you are a leader, you may identify with some of the issues described. If you are a team member, you probably relate to some of these issues or work for a leader who demonstrates several of these behaviors.

I am not implying that leading people is a walk in the park—it takes patience, understanding and compassion. I am well aware that some employees complain and take advantage of their leader's kindness. As a result, a leader may become calloused. Nonetheless, I also appreciate that it is even more challenging to work for leaders, or have colleagues, who are not kindhearted.

In any case, whether you are a leader or a team member, listen with an effort to understand, instead of making assumptions or judging. Leaders, even though you are the ones in charge, stop bossing people around. Instead, treat your team members with respect and as fellow human beings. Most importantly, if your actions do not feel right, don't take that route. You will not regret your decision.

Ovsan

CHAPTER I

Us vs. Them

Nearly all men can stand adversity, but if you want to test a man's character, give him power.

—Abraham Lincoln

In the various positions I have held throughout my career, it seemed as though there was always a dichotomy between leaders and team members. There was a mentality of "us versus them." The expectation was that team members were to follow the leaders without those two positions ever connecting. What I mean is that, most of the time the common practice was that leaders were the ones who gave the orders to the rest of the team, telling them what to do. After all, they were the ones with the position and power. And, in turn, the team members were to quietly conform to their leaders' every request without objection or questioning. Leaders rarely asked for input from their workers who may have had suggestions or ideas that could have improved the process or the end result of a product.

The other concept was that leaders were to keep their distance from their team, maintaining an image of sternness and strictness. It was important to enforce a certain remoteness that established the "us versus them" mentality. It was not considered appropriate for leaders to befriend their subordinates, because getting too close to their people could weaken their power. Consequently, they could lose their control over the team.

Looking back at all those years, as well as my personal experiences and observations, I now can confidently say that these concepts are completely unreasonable and objectionable. The "us versus them" mentality is unnecessary and should not exist. Instead, leaders need to cultivate an atmosphere of teamwork and cohesion where everyone has a voice and is able to share opinions and suggestions without fear of retaliation.

Leaders can only succeed in leading a team if there is cohesion between them and their team members. First of all, where would a leader be if he or she didn't have a team to lead? And, how could a team accomplish results without a strong leader? A leader is needed to ensure everyone is moving along in the same direction, achieving the goals and vision of a company. And, a good team is important to be able to get the job done on time, accurately and on budget. The bottom line is that, to be successful, leaders and team members must collaborate.

> *Leaders can only succeed in leading a team if there's cohesion between them and their team members.*

You did, I didn't

Have you ever worked for a leader who was so quick to point a finger at you when you made a mistake that even the thought of possibly making a mistake paralyzed you?

And, how about a leader who denied what he or she said, making it sound as if the error was all because you did not follow directions? Typical reactions might be, "I don't remember saying that;" "That's not what I said;" or "You understood incorrectly."

What about the leader who left you hanging in the midst of a problem so that you had to resolve the issue by yourself, without giving you any support?

Oh, and let's not forget the leader who asked for your input on an issue, but when you shared your thoughts and opinion, your feedback was later held against you. Perhaps you were told you were not cooperating or you were not supporting your leader's vision.

No wonder there's a sense of "us versus them"! The "us" (leaders) tend to point the finger at "them" (team members) instead of joining forces, coming together as equals and trying to resolve issues for the benefit of all involved.

Certainly, you can relate to what I'm saying here. And, interestingly enough, I am sure you can spot these characteristics and behaviors not only in your immediate superiors, but also in your peers and colleagues, friends, and maybe even family members.

Sincerity matters

Over the years, I've met and worked for various leaders as I've moved up in my career path. Whether I reported to these leaders directly, worked with them on cross-functional projects, or heard stories from colleagues, it didn't quite matter. After interacting with them for a while, I was able to see past their façade and figure out whether they were being sincere in their words and actions, or if they were simply being pretentious. Their true thoughts and intentions were obvious to me, as I could feel what they held in their hearts—reading through the lines of fake smiles and compliments.

See, I think of myself as someone with a strong intuition, with the ability to read others' intentions, ultimately uncovering their true selves, be they good or bad. Unfortunately, this skill can be a curse as much as it can be considered a gift. On many occasions, even though certain leaders presented a cheerful front with the pretense of having a true interest in me, it didn't take me long to see their hidden agendas, dishonesty, or insecurities. This perceptiveness, instinct, gut feeling, or whatever you'd like to call it, has helped me throughout the years as I've adapted to new management styles and expectations.

I've had leaders who were so opinionated that it was as though they had blinders on and were unable to see beyond their own thoughts and ideas. Generally, their body language was louder than their spoken words, and conveyed a message of, "Who are you to tell me why my approach is not the best?!"

I remember, years ago I was assigned to a project led by a person who was new to the company. As we were getting into the thick of things on the project, we reached a point where we had to determine how to manage a problem we were having. Given that I had worked on other related projects several times before and had overcome similar issues, I tried explaining and providing suggestions on how to resolve this problem. Unfortunately, my advice fell on deaf ears—to the detriment of the company. The project fell through, more funds were spent to rectify the issue, and, eventually, we had to approach the issue the way I had originally suggested.

The lesson to be learned here is that, as a leader, it's crucial to set your ego aside and truly listen to a team member, especially if this person has more experience than you in that area. Ignoring his or her input may cause you to end up going down a path that has already proven to be a dead end in the past. Not only will the company suffer, but you will also lose the trust and respect of your team members.

My way or the highway

How about those leaders who are obstinate, with closed vision, no sense of risk management, and are unable to admit they made a mistake? It's their way or the highway! Yes, you know the kind I'm talking about. The funny and yet sad thing about these types of leaders is that, even when they know they have made a mistake, they are never willing to admit it and say, "I'm sorry."

Throughout the years, I've observed several leaders with these characteristics. One of them has made a lifelong impact on me. This leader was notorious for giving instructions. But later, when things didn't work out, he would lie through his teeth and blame everyone else without ever admitting that he may have just made a bad decision, or was simply wrong.

As a leader, admitting you've made a mistake is incredibly important—that's how you will earn your team's trust and respect. We all make mistakes. No one is perfect. Just because you are the leader doesn't mean that you should have all the answers. The important thing is to admit it and learn from your mistakes so you don't repeat them in the future.

We'll talk about these attributes in greater detail in the next chapter.

> *Just because you are the leader doesn't mean that you should have all the answers.*

When things get tough

I could list a multitude of leadership behaviors and traits that generate unnecessary friction and misunderstandings amongst the team, resulting in conflict and the dichotomy of "us versus them" we talked about earlier.

To name just a few of these behaviors: egocentric, venal, rude, condescending, ungrateful, unrealistic, lack of perspective, unappreciative, disrespectful, taking credit for a subordinate's (or someone else's) work. And, this list could go on and on. I don't doubt that you could add a few more adjectives to this list from your own experiences.

All of the above are connected to the same issue: having a big ego and the inability to apologize when things go wrong. Another likely situation that may arise from this issue is your team members making a mistake because of your misdirection. Instead of owning the problem, you abandon them, leaving them to deal with it. When you, as a leader, are not supportive or do not stand behind your people, and you leave them hanging during tough times, the entire energy and morale of the work environment changes. You lose your team's respect and trust. And, next time they have to do something for you, they'll hesitate in case you back out if things go south.

During these tough times when projects go amiss, it's important to put your ego aside, take charge of your feelings and emotions and realize that your behavior is crucial to the success of your team.

There is a clear pattern that can be observed with these types of leaders who are always wavering and blaming others for their failures. They are often insecure in their own skin, and the only way they know how to continue to pretend they are in control is by acting out and belittling others. Other negative behaviors can include: being rude or abrupt when dealing with their team, giving them inappropriate feedback about their performance, or taking credit for their team's work. These behaviors give weak leaders a false sense of security and superiority.

If you're at the receiving end of these behaviors, try not to let them get under your skin. Take any feedback into consideration and see whether there's a growth opportunity for you. But, at all times, keep in mind that you know who you are and what you stand for. Obviously, your leader can help you grow or just as easily have you fired. So, you have to make a decision: either suck it up and go with the flow, or take charge of things. Weigh the pros and cons and decide whether it's worth your effort to confront your leader with the issue or to quietly start looking for a new job.

They do exist

Having said all of the above, I'm also aware that there are leaders who genuinely care about their team, who understand that everyone makes mistakes, and that people are not without flaws. No one is perfect, right? And yet, why is it that the minute a mistake is made, everyone seems to go crazy? My philosophy is that unless the mistake is a life-or-death situation, affects someone's livelihood, or ruins someone's reputation, nothing else is worth losing sleep over. As the saying goes, "To err is human, to forgive…divine!"

I've seen leaders who had a great sense of humor, leaders who knew when to be serious, but also when to make light of things and move on. They were eager to support and serve their team members and were always open to new ideas and suggestions. Most importantly, they were willing and ready to learn from their team members.

As a leader, it's essential for you to be understanding and realize that your team is made up of human beings who are just like you. They have similar feelings and thoughts and want to be treated with respect and dignity. As a team member, if you're fortunate enough to have a leader who has these attributes, stick with him or her—leaders with a heart are fast becoming a rare species in the workplace. The culprit, in my opinion, is the fact that companies are promoting or hiring people in leadership roles who are not ready to lead. Generally, these new leaders are more interested in their own achievements and growth rather than inspiring and mentoring their team. In other words, their motives are not always genuine. They have their own hidden agendas. And, most notably, they lack the soft skills essential for leaders to succeed.

> *As a leader, it's essential for you to be understanding and realize that your team is made up of human beings who are just like you.*

Why they are the way they are

As I've observed several managers and leaders over the years, I've come to realize that most undesirable leadership characteristics stem from people's insecurities, their personal experiences and life circumstances. Usually, their upbringing, the environment in which they were raised and their current family life make a huge difference in how they behave at work.

As I look back at each one of the leaders with whom I had the pleasure of working (and yes, now looking back, I can say it was a pleasure getting to know all the different personalities and characteristics), they all taught me something along the way, consciously or unconsciously, simply by being themselves. Some of these leaders taught me how to behave as a leader, and others taught me how not to act. Being at the receiving end, these experiences were invaluable for me. I owe them all a great deal. Had I not worked with the bad leaders, I wouldn't be able to appreciate the good leaders who came along.

Two types of leaders

Leaders can be categorized into two main types: (1) those who are authoritarian and generally overconfident, leading with force and arrogance; and (2) those who are servant leaders filled with compassion and are caring, but still confident in what they know—able to direct and empower their team to grow in their roles.

When asked which type of a leader would be most successful in getting things done, some people believe that force is essential to prompt their team into action. Attributes such as kindness, caring and understanding generally fall to the sidelines and are looked upon as weaknesses rather than strengths in a leader. But, let me ask you this: Would you rather work for a leader who is egocentric, inconsiderate and impolite or one who is kind, supporting, caring and understanding? I think I already know your answer.

Overconfidence doesn't help

As a leader, you have to be confident in your own knowledge and skills, but careful not to come across as cocky. Know what you do and keep yourself up-to-speed on what's happening in your industry as well as new technology that you may need in order to continue to be efficient in your position. This is important for your growth because, as you develop yourself, those who work with you or who report to you directly will also benefit from your experiences and knowledge. Your positive energy will become contagious, influencing your team to do more and keep an upbeat attitude even when things get tough.

One of the mistakes leaders generally make is becoming too comfortable in their position, which leads them to stop cultivating their expertise about what's going on in their industry. This puts them in a vulnerable position, resulting in insecurities and doubt in their own abilities.

When you as a leader do not continue your own growth and develop your skills, either by reading what's relevant in your industry or by engaging in current activities that pertain to your position, you may feel you're losing that leadership edge. You may find yourself surrounded by colleagues, subordinates, or senior leaders who now know more than you do (or maybe they pretend they know what they are doing and are believable). That feeling alone may make you uncomfortable, causing

> *One of the mistakes leaders generally make is becoming too comfortable in their position.*

you to start doubting yourself. As a result, you may become paranoid and suspicious of everyone around you. You may wonder if anyone's trying to sabotage your work, or feel that a colleague might be stabbing you in the back. Even worse, you may think he or she is trying to make your life miserable enough so you'll quit, allowing him or her to quickly move in and take over your position.

Are there boundaries?

As we discussed earlier, leaders often fall prey to the misconception that they should create a delineation of "us versus them," thus keeping distance between themselves and their teams. This behavior benefits no one. On the contrary, it creates a dichotomy affecting the synchronicity of the team.

A true leader has the ability to read people and understand when to help and when to push for results. A true leader is able to open up and invite his or her people to share their own thoughts and ideas, ensuring everyone has the opportunity to feel they are part of the effort at hand. Ultimately, this will create a better product. You've heard of the saying, "Two heads are better than one." Well, it's true when it comes to teamwork.

Unfortunately, there are colleagues or subordinates who are malicious, jealous and full of bitterness from prior experiences. Because of this, they try to harm others for their own benefit, not caring how many "dead bodies" they leave around them as they climb the leadership ladder. However, their glory and fame is limited, because eventually their karma does come back to haunt them. It's important for leaders to be aware of these types of people and work with them, helping them to realize that they're part of a team designed to support and help each other work through difficulties and achieve common goals.

Generally, when a leader shows compassion and understanding toward a team member who is going through a tough time, that team member will turn around and start respecting and looking up to his or her leader.

Is hard work enough?

When you've worked almost all your life, as I have, you tend to become calloused toward the not-so-pleasant workplace experiences. I've been working since the age of 17, and am still at it. I remember my first job as a telex telephone operator. Some of you reading this may not even know what a telex is, especially if you belong to the post-1970s generation. Just think of it as an archaic way of text messaging using typewriters. It took agility to operate the telex machine while managing incoming calls, and yet, somehow I coped with it pretty well. I not only mastered the job, but was promoted to an administrative position in less than six months. I know it doesn't sound too exciting now, but at the time, as a 17-year-old young girl, I was thrilled to be recognized as a hard worker and given the opportunity to learn something new. And, it didn't stop there. Soon after, I was offered the position of executive assistant to the managing director of the company. At age 20, I was already supervising two assistants. I was lucky to have had one of the best leaders as my manager. He was understanding, caring, funny, and had a kind heart. Although at times we did disagree, he never held any of that against me. Instead, he valued my input and appreciated that I had the guts to stand up for what I believed to be true or better for the company.

Back then, being an executive assistant was not as simple as some people may think. These assistants were expected to do all sorts of odd jobs, which in today's workplace, would be considered discriminatory or borderline sexual harassment. To give you an example, part of my regular duties included attending meetings and taking minutes. This involved using shorthand to take notes as my boss dictated various letters, which I would then transcribe for his signature, after editing his words and proofing the final typed copy. But, on top of all that, I remember one of my daily chores was to make my boss' coffee, clean up and tidy his office, and dust his desk. At times, I'd even make arrangements for his personal appointments.

As I gained more experience with the work, I became more confident and started asking more questions, challenging certain decisions my manager would make. I now understand that sometimes I may have been crossing the line as I tried to share my point of view a bit too forcefully. But, I also remember my manager being understanding, explaining the reasoning behind his decisions, and guiding me in the right direction so I could learn and grow. He knew that by helping me flourish, he was actually working toward making his life easier. After a while, he didn't even have to dictate any letters or tell me how to write them. I already knew what to say and what not to say. Eventually, I got to the point where I was able to write his letters and he would simply sign them. Now, that's an investment he made in me as he mentored me and allowed me to grow in my position. I never once felt any resentment or pushback from him. Instead, he was a leader who knew his strengths, and I looked up to him knowing that he would be there for me no matter what. This was a win-win working relationship.

However, along the way, I realized that hard work was not always enough. I had to learn each person's likes and dislikes. I had to manage personalities to make sure we had a harmonious atmosphere in the workplace. As I grew in my position, it became obvious to me that in order to succeed, I had to know when to speak up and when to just nod and agree, even if I didn't quite see eye-to-eye with my manager. And, later on as a manager myself, I began to understand how it felt to walk in those shoes.

The bottom line is that, if, as a leader, you gain the trust and respect of your team and are sought out for your knowledge, expertise and support, your team will be loyal to you, knowing that you will be there to guide and lead them to success. In return, the positive synergy of your team will make you feel secure and confident no matter what the outcome of any situation may be.

Keep in mind that regardless of how much work you have on your plate or how mundane you consider certain tasks to be, your staff needs your guidance and support. As you help them succeed, you're actually benefiting yourself as a leader. When your team performs at its best and accomplishes goals, their success reflects positively on you, showing you to be a leader who knows how to keep a team motivated.

Colleagues vs. friends and family

During various leadership training and management courses we are told that it is necessary to separate our work life from our personal life. We need to differentiate where one stops and the other starts. I completely agree that there needs to be a balance between how many hours we put into our work and how much time we devote to having some fun with our loved ones. But, whether you're dealing with colleagues, friends or family members, the expectations are similar.

Before you react or disagree with this statement, just answer this question: What qualities do you look for in your colleagues or staff? Take a minute and write down what comes to mind. Now, think about the qualities you cherish in a friend or a family member. Take one more minute to write down those qualities. Lastly, compare your two lists. What do you see?

I bet your two lists have several similarities between them. That's because there is not much difference between what we look for in a team member or a colleague and what we would like to see from our friends or family members. Just think about it, most of us spend eight or more hours each day with our colleagues and staff, which is generally more time than we spend with our friends and family.

I suspect you would want your friends and family members to be loyal, caring, trustworthy, respectful, appreciative, honest, and be there for you when you need them. Well, aren't these expectations similar to what you would expect from your colleagues and team members? Wouldn't you want a team that is loyal to you, supports you, cares for and respects you, and is there for you when you need help to get the job done?

Having said that, I realize it is not always possible to be close friends with everyone at work. It's inevitable that you won't be able to get along with every single colleague or a team member—some may challenge you or irritate you. But isn't that true with family members or relatives? Do you really love all of your family members? I bet there are those whom you can't stand either, but you just learn to live with them.

So, my question to you is this: Why the disparity of treatment between coworkers and friends or family members? Why the separation? Don't you think that the closer you are to your team, the better the communication channels, the stronger the connection and the easier and quicker work is accomplished? You may be thinking, "What if they take advantage of my kindheartedness and don't follow through with my directions? What if they do not respect me as their leader?" This is where I have a fundamental difference of opinion. My personal experience has been that when you are closer and friendlier with the team, you get more work out of them, and they do it because they **want to**, not because they **have to**.

Leader vs. parent

The relationship of a leader with his or her team can also be characterized as that between parents with their children. I can hear you thinking, "I am their leader, not their parent!" Don't misunderstand me. When I compare leadership to parenthood, this is what I mean: there needs to be open and direct communication among you, and your team should feel comfortable enough to share any concerns or problems with you rather than be scared of your power. Fear and respect are two very different things. When someone fears you because you're in a certain position, that is not an indication of respect toward you, or of you being a good leader. On the contrary, it means that you are most likely so distant from what is really happening at the team level that you are not able to identify with the real issues. If your team fears you, then they will continue to say, "yes" to you no matter what they may be thinking.

The same concept also applies to parenthood. As a parent, if your children are afraid of you, that doesn't mean they respect you. On the contrary, they will lie to you through their teeth just to get away with something or to avoid confrontation. If your child is in trouble, wouldn't you want him or her to come and tell you what's going on so you can help and guide him or her before it's too late?

It's exactly the same situation with your team members. If you have an open relationship where you can talk about anything, then your team members will feel at ease sharing any concerns they have with you, and together, you'll be able to sort things out. Otherwise, they'll nod and smile to your face, but complain behind your back about what an incompetent and insensitive leader you are. That is not the type of reputation you want to have.

By being connected with the team on their level, you automatically create a bond. They know you're there to support and help them no matter what may happen.

> *By being connected with the team on their level, you automatically create a bond*

Keep it real

The more open, genuine and honest you are with your staff, the more respected you will be as their leader. I understand that, at times, leaders have to play organizational politics, but there's a limit to it all. If you don't agree with a decision made by your superiors but are obligated to implement it, obviously you have to keep a positive attitude as a leader so as not to negatively influence your team. But, at the same time, it's important to keep it real and realize that people can read through the lines. If they see you pretending to ignore the obvious and trying to convince them that a certain decision is the right one, even though that may not be the case, you will lose your team's respect, and your credibility will suffer.

I am sure you agree that everyone has a boss. Even the president and the CEO of a company have to report to the board of directors or the shareholders of the company. We all have to answer to someone, be it at work or at home. Following the directions you receive from your superiors and yet simultaneously keeping your management style authentic and real for your team are two different things.

Here's how you can do both:

1. Explain the situation to the team as best you can by sharing the details that you know, and rationalizing the leadership decision.

2. Let your team know that while you understand that not all of the decisions made by the leadership may make sense to them, sometimes that may be because we may not have the complete picture of why or how certain decisions are made. Therefore we need to stand behind our leaders' decisions.

Through this honest and candid approach, your team will feel respected and will be comfortable in executing what's expected of them to meet the overall organizational goals.

POWER vs. *Heart* in Leadership

CHAPTER II

The H -E -A -R -T of the Matter

A leader is best when people barely know he exists. When his work is done, his aim fulfilled, they will say: we did it ourselves.

–Lao Tzu

For as long as I can remember, I have been a strong believer in the idea that it is important to be kind to everyone, being mindful not to intentionally hurt people's feelings. Even as a child, it bothered me when I witnessed someone being mistreated by another person. I just could not understand why some people were mean and seemed to enjoy putting others down, only to satisfy their own egos or make themselves feel more powerful and in control.

In retrospect, I feel pity for these types of people. I now realize they have no connection with their inner self. These are people who have low self-esteem and a false sense of self-confidence. And, lamentably, the only way they know how to feel good about themselves is by projecting their own shortcomings onto others. That's why, as hard as it may be, it's vital to remind ourselves to be understanding and patient when confronted with people who display these characteristics.

Yes, I know it's not always easy to be tolerant and empathetic, especially when people constantly rub you the wrong way or try to hurt you no matter how nice you are to them. But, those are the instances when you are truly tested as a human being. Are you able to control yourself, maintain your composure and continue to be kind no matter how others act? Or, do you succumb to your emotions and get dirty with them?

The whole purpose of our life is to live as human beings who are kind, considerate, loving and supportive of each other. We need to open our hearts to those around us, helping them feel safe, valued and comfortable enough to express their thoughts and opinions without fear of retaliation. We need to think about how we can be a blessing to those we encounter and have a positive influence in their lives. This should be our ultimate goal no matter what the circumstances. Keep in mind that when we're being nice to someone, we are actually being nice to ourselves—we're creating good karma that will come back to find us sooner or later.

> *The whole purpose of our life is to live as human beings who are kind, considerate, loving and supportive of each other.*

Just think for a second. What would we gain by hurting others, or by being rude and arrogant? In our work environment, instead of helping the situation, we would be creating a place of chaos and bad energy where no one is productive or happy. On the other hand, good synergy and a pleasant atmosphere can change things for the better. I am sure you've heard of the saying, "Have a heart." And, that's exactly what you need in order to succeed, not only as a leader, but also as a human being here on this earth for such a limited period of time. Our life is nothing but a brief parenthesis in the vast scope of things. If we kept things in perspective, then nothing would be important enough to make us be discourteous, disrespectful or mean to our fellow humans.

To succeed as a leader, you must treasure certain characteristics. In this chapter, I'd like to discuss the five most important human attributes you need as a leader. If you haven't guessed it already, all of these attributes are connected to your heart, your inner self, your gut feeling, or True Self. No matter what you call it, these are the elements that will make you stand out as a leader who cares for and understands his or her team members.

Five attributes of the H -E -A -R -T

When you think of the word heart, what comes to mind? Do you think of the internal organ that's no bigger than the size of your fist, and yet continuously pumps without missing a beat 24 hours a day to ensure blood is flowing throughout your body? Do you think of cupid, romance or love? Or, maybe does the word heart for you bring up feelings of pain and suffering because someone broke your heart, and you've never been able to pick up the pieces?

All of the above are valid thoughts, but I'd like to introduce you to a new concept as to what having a heart means for a leader. You may think these associations are cheesy or obvious, yet many leaders lack more than one of these attributes. As a result, we see unsatisfied, disgruntled employees full of resentment and low morale, all of which lead to frequent staff turnover and unhealthy work environments.

Let's review each one of these five attributes.

H-E-A-R-T = *H*umility

Having a certain rank or position in an organization, or being promoted to that senior leadership level, doesn't mean that you have the right to demoralize or look down on those who are now below you. Even if you are promoted to be a CEO or vice president of a company, the position alone doesn't make you a better person. All it means is that you now have more power over others and you know something different than someone else.

The bottom line is that you, just like the person answering the phones or cleaning the restrooms, are one and the same. You all come from the same source and will end up at the same source. You are all human beings on this earth with similar hardships, experiences, sadness, wants and desires. But, you just happen to hold different positions in a company. If you switched positions for a day, I am sure that you, as the CEO, would have a hard time handling those phones efficiently, or making sure those toilets were spic and span, just as the person answering the phones or cleaning the restrooms wouldn't be able to handle the responsibilities that come with your position without the proper education, training and years of experience. And yet, you are a human being, as are they.

It is undeniable that CEOs and vice presidents fall apart without their assistants—they often don't know the first thing about how to book a meeting or create a PowerPoint presentation that looks halfway decent. My point is everyone in a company has certain experience or knowledge that another doesn't. So, everyone deserves the respect and appreciation of everyone else, regardless of their position.

It takes humility for a CEO or vice president to put his or her position power aside and approach his or her people with an open mind. You have to remember that, no matter how much education you have or what level your position is, you can always learn something new from another person, no matter his or her status in life or his or her rank in your company. The more humble you are in your position, the more you'll be respected, not only as a leader, but also as a human being.

> *The more humble you are in your position, the more you'll be respected, not only as a leader, but also as a human being.*

But, let's make it clear that being humble does not mean you need to become a rug, allowing everyone to walk all over you. On the contrary, it means that you, as a leader, realize that everyone is a human being, an individual who deserves to be treated with respect.

As their leader, you listen to what your people have to share. You approach situations with no preconceptions or predispositions. You are open to suggestions and willing to admit you are wrong when you make a mistake. What a concept, eh? It also means admitting when you make a mistake, or when your idea may not have been the best one after all. Throughout my career, I've encountered leaders who were so full of themselves that they never said they were sorry, even if I presented concrete proof that what they were saying was wrong.

What really puzzled me were leaders who, after being promoted to senior levels, passed by me without a smile or "Hello." I'm talking about leaders with whom I had worked for years before they were promoted to their higher positions. This is where humility comes in once again. Saying, "Hello" with a smile to the people you work with goes a long way. Your pleasant and friendly attitude makes them feel valued and appreciated. And, having a smile on your face makes you feel good, too. So, it's a win-win situation. Don't be that leader who is stuck up and believes that everyone needs to obey your every command! My grandmother used to say, "A 'hello' comes from heaven." In other words, we should always greet those who cross our paths with a smile, even if we don't know them, because that's the humane thing to do. It doesn't cost us anything, and yet it may brighten someone's life.

Holding a senior-level position unquestionably requires more focus and comes with accountability. This accountability not only includes the success of the organization and meeting set goals, but also the company's employees. Every decision you make affects many people and their families. Unfortunately, at times, leaders at a certain level in an organization become conceited and full of themselves, and their decisions become based on, "What's in it for me?" instead of, "What's best for the company as well as the team?"

The minute these types of people find themselves in a powerful leadership position, their behavior toward their colleagues and subordinates changes. Now they see themselves as being above everyone else and having the ability to control and manipulate them as they please. But, the truly successful leaders are the ones who are prepared to serve instead of being served. As Lao Tzu, the ancient Chinese philosopher said, and I am paraphrasing, to lead means being a servant to those beneath them, helping them grow and flourish.

H- *E* -A-R-T = **Equality**

One of the biggest gaffes a leader can make is playing favorites. How did it make you feel when you could sense that your mother was giving more attention to your sibling? Sad, betrayed, disappointed? Maybe you were thinking, "What's wrong with me? What am I doing wrong?" Needless to say, playing favorites in the workplace can have the same effect on your team members.

Understandably, as a leader, it's possible that you may enjoy working with a certain individual more than another. You may have a deeper connection with one person versus another. You may have one team member who walks on water, yet another who needs constant handholding. Perhaps a team member rubs you the wrong way, or another tries to brownnose you all the time. Regardless of the situation, or how you feel toward your team members, it's essential that you treat all of them equally.

Now, you may be thinking, "How can I treat everyone equally if one person is performing better than the other?" Let me share a few scenarios to help explain what I mean.

~Scenario I~

Let's assume you have one person on your team, whom we will call Susan for the purpose of this example. Susan is always late in the mornings, and doesn't stay late to make up the time. Yet you don't discipline or talk to Susan about her attendance because you are friends outside of the workplace. And, you also happen to know that she's going through some family issues. Even worse, you justify Susan's tardiness to your team when this is brought to your attention. You make excuses for her and allow this behavior to continue. On the other hand, you have another team member, whom we shall call Sarah, who starts having attendance issues as well. You notice Sarah coming in late in the mornings, but stays late to make up her time. And yet, instead of trying to understand the reason behind her tardiness, you call her into your office and lecture her on attendance and the importance of coming to work on time.

Can you see how these two team members are not being treated equally here? If you allow one of your team members to be late to work—for whatever reason—you cannot discipline another for being late especially when this person is staying late to make up the time. That's not the behavior of a leader who treats the team with equality. Your team definitely notices that Susan gets away with coming in late every day, yet they hear you gave Sarah a hard time because she started coming in late. This differentiation of treatment amongst the group will create a negative atmosphere and a sense of resentment between your team members and toward you.

~Scenario II~

One team member—let's call him John—doesn't seem to be able to have his work done in a timely manner. He always misses deadlines, and when he presents his work, it's generally not in a final format. He asks very basic questions, which, at his level and years of experience, he should be able to handle on his own. Yet, you are very understanding with John. You coach him, help him finalize his work, and hold his hand throughout the project. And, once the project is done, you even give him a bonus for a job well done, even though the delivery was poor and far from being timely.

Now, on the other hand, you have another team member whom you don't like very much—let's call her

Martha. Martha has a project that is similar to John's and just as complicated. She has been able to move things along as much as she can and is doing a great job. When she comes in to ask you a question, you are abrupt with your answers. You don't take the time to discuss the issues or try to help her. Instead, you tell her she is at a level where she should be able to handle these issues on her own. You brush her off, come to conclusions on your own, and tell her how disappointed you are by the quality of her work, and that, no matter how hard she tried, she'd never excel.

Now, let's examine this scenario. John comes to you with questions and asks for help. Martha does the same. But, John, whom you like better, gets your attention and direction; yet you tell Martha to go and find the information on her own. Again, there is a distinct inequality in how these two team members are treated.

Do you think even for a moment that Martha won't feel the disparity in treatment? No matter how discrete you may think you're being with your conversations with your team, trust me, they will talk behind your back. So, eventually it will be no secret that John and Martha are being held to different standards.

And what will that do to your team's spirit and morale if you keep this up? Nothing good will come out of it—I can assure you of that. There will be resentment toward you as a leader. You will lose your team's respect and loyalty. Your high-performing employees will start looking for other opportunities, leaving you with the poor performers.

When a leader starts to play favorites, it encourages the formation of cliques in the department. The cliques will comprise those who are the leader's protégés and those who are treated as stepchildren. As a result, feelings of antipathy, hostility, anger, disappointment and dissatisfaction start to increase. The team doesn't get along. They talk behind each other's back. They don't want to help each other. They may even start to withhold information from each other. Eventually, all of these behaviors and incidents start affecting productivity, and mistakes happen. Those treated as stepchildren may lose interest in their work. You may notice that there are frequent missed deadlines and that the quality of service is suffering. Each conversation ends up in a misunderstanding, and, worst of all, colleagues start looking at your favorites or protégés with bitterness.

The sad part is that, generally, the team members who are favored and protected by the leader are not very ecstatic about the better treatment either. Similar to being the teacher's pet, the protégés sense the resentment from their colleagues, which puts them in an awkward situation. The result: none of your team members are happy any longer, and the work environment becomes toxic. All of this just because you, as their leader, did not treat them fairly and equally.

> *Treat everyone equally to maintain the harmony and peace in the department.*

Next time you have an issue at hand, before you dismiss it, think about what type of precedence you may be setting, or what unpleasant message you are sending to the rest of the group. Treat everyone equally to maintain the harmony and peace in the department.

H-E-*A*-R-T = *Appreciation*

It's not just what you teach your team that makes a lasting impression, it's how you make them feel along the way. Your words must be sincere, honest and come from your heart.

When things don't go as planned, your team looks up to you as their leader and expects your support, guidance and understanding. How you react to situations will affect how the team views you as a leader. Remember, your every move is always being watched and judged. You are your team's mirror and role model. If you expect your team to work hard, make sure you're meeting your own deadlines, and go above and beyond expectations.

As you work together toward meeting those tight deadlines, solving problems and clearing obstacles, and you reach the peak moment when everything is going crazy, it's important to let your team know they are appreciated. Tell them how much you value their hard work and dedication. Don't wait until you complete the project. Take the time to celebrate the progress they make. Know that their insight and focused minds are important to the success of the project. If you don't encourage them as you move through each phase of the project and confirm that you value their efforts, you run the risk of your team members losing their excitement, because eventually their energy and dedication to the project will decrease.

Sometimes all it takes is a simple heartfelt "Thank you!" You may not realize it, but a sincere expression of gratitude goes a long way. When you appreciate their hard work, they feel valued and this motivates them to try harder next time, surmounting any obstacles they may face. Be mindful, however, how and when you say, "Thank you." If you constantly say it, even if the job was not up to your expectations, you devalue the message it sends. Make sure you say it only when the effort really deserves it. Remember, the most

> *You may not realize it, but a sincere "thank you" goes a long way.*

important thing to keep in mind is to be genuine and authentic in whatever you say. Make sure you show your appreciation sincerely and in a timely manner.

Appreciation and performance

As a leader reading this book, you may be thinking, "How can I appreciate a person when he or she doesn't give 100 percent to the project, makes mistakes, or doesn't always meet deadlines?" My questions back to you are: Why is there such a person on your team in the first place? What have you done to address this problem? Have you made an effort to find out more about what's going on in this person's life that may be affecting his or her work? Have you ever thought that maybe—just maybe—**you** may also be the cause for some of the issues you're having with that person?

To help you answer your questions, here's a list of possibilities that may be at the root of this person's poor performance:

1. A personal or family reason

2. A health issue either with him or her, or a family member

3. A conflict amongst colleagues that is causing intimidation or low morale

4. A lack of knowledge or training to do the job right

5. Inadequate resources to accomplish the job

6. A lack of cooperation from other cross-functional areas that may need your nudging

7. And, maybe the most difficult possibility: you, as the leader. Do you make yourself available to answer questions to help this person move the project along when faced with a roadblock?

Before you start making assumptions or judgments about a person, your duty as a leader is to have a heart-to-heart conversation with this team member to ensure you're not overlooking something important.

Poor performance does not always mean that an individual is a bad employee or that he or she doesn't care. A greater underlying problem may be affecting this person's performance and disrupting his or her daily routine. Once you choose to be open and honest with the person, you will be amazed and pleasantly surprised at how you can touch this person's heart and turn him or her around. I am not saying this shift will happen overnight. It takes a lot of hard work, patience and perseverance as a leader in order to gain your team's trust. If it were easy, everyone would be able to do this. It takes a heart to understand, sympathize with, and encourage the person to do his or her best.

In order to bring the best out of a team member, when things are not going well, it's important to have those tough conversations in private when things are not going well. When you notice that one of your good performers starts to produce mediocre work, your first step, not only as a leader but as a human being who cares about another person's well-being, is to meet with that individual, preferably away from your office, and try to understand if there is anything you can do to help him or her. Don't make assumptions. Take the time to listen and understand where he or she is coming from.

Years ago, a friend shared with me a story that I'll never forget. To date, it gives me goose bumps when I think about it. I'd like to share this experience with you as an indication of how reaching out to a person can be the best thing you can do as a leader.

> *One of the receptionists at a local company—let's call her Joanne—didn't show up for work one morning. No one knew where she was or why she hadn't come in. Joanne didn't call in, nor did she pick up her phone. The next day, Joanne came in as usual. Her leader, let's call him Jack, full of fury and eager to exercise his position power, called Joanne into his office. Before even asking why she didn't come to work the day before, Jack started reprimanding her, telling her how irresponsible it was on her part not to have called in. He reminded her about the company policy*

that a "no call, no show" may result in immediate termination. After going on for a while, Jack finally said to Joanne in a stern voice, "What do you have to say for yourself?" Joanne looked at Jack with a gloomy look on her face as if a dark cloud was hanging over her head. With tears in her eyes and a trembling voice, she said, "I'm sorry I didn't call you, but yesterday morning both my parents were killed in a car accident." At that moment, Jack felt smaller than the smallest insect on the face of the planet. He choked and couldn't utter a single word. He felt like an idiot and vowed on that day that he would never again make an assumption—that he would always allow the person to explain him or herself before sharing a piece of his mind.

You see, as leaders, sometimes we are quick to assume the worst based on certain behaviors. But, we need to treat each incidence as a separate event. First, try to understand what the reason is. Then, try to help and guide. Show your appreciation often and be sincere about it. Your kind words alone will go a long way with your team.

Words can kill

We have talked about how you, as a leader, can help motivate and encourage your low performers to increase their confidence by providing support, guidance and patience as you show them the way. At the same time, I don't want to disregard the fact that you may be demoralizing your high-performing team members without even

> *First, try to understand what the reason is. Then, try to help and guide.*

realizing it. How you communicate with your team is critical. Each word you use is powerful, and, if you aren't careful, these words can work to your team's detriment. So, it's crucial to pick your words mindfully, asking the right questions so as not to make a team member feel unappreciated or undermine the work he or she does.

Before you start criticizing how something is being handled or start to micromanage, first learn about the details of a project, including the time and effort needed to accomplish the deliverables. Most often, when a task gets done fast and without any complications, leaders make the assumption that it must have been an easy endeavor. Keep in mind that if, on the surface, the work at hand does not appear to be complex, it may be due to your employee's experience, knowledge, and ability to anticipate and manage risks—handling them before they become issues.

Here's an example of what I mean:

A leader insisted that a project his team was working on was very simple. When the team tried to explain to him that there were many dependencies and prongs to the project as well as several other contributors who delayed its progress, he refused to try to understand. All the team heard back was, "It shouldn't take this long. I've worked on more complicated projects, and I did it in less time and with less people." This statement, mind you, came from a leader who had been in his position for only two months. As you can imagine, his attitude was demoralizing. The team felt as if he was completely dismissing and devaluing all of the hard work and time they had been investing in this project for more than 10 years.

The lesson to learn here is to think before you open your mouth. As a leader, choose your words and the tone you use carefully, because you can make or break your team's spirit based on how you approach each situation. If you're faced with a situation similar to the example above where you think your team may be working slower than you would like on a certain project, take a moment to think before you intervene. Try to understand the process and the complexity involved, especially if you were never personally involved in the details of the project.

Creative appreciation

For the past several years, because of the economy, companies are watching their expenses, and cost savings has become a focal point for the success of the business. Budgets are being cut, and leaders are asked to accomplish more with less. You may be facing this situation as well and thinking, "How do I show my appreciation to my team when I don't have a budget for it?"

Appreciation can come in various forms. As a leader, you have to get creative and think outside the box. As I mentioned earlier, money is not always the sole motivator for people to try harder and excel in what they do. Yes, it sure does help when there's a nice bonus involved, or when a huge raise is on the horizon. But, in most cases, what drives people the most is a sense of belonging and the feeling that they are playing an important part in the team's success. They want to experience and feel in their hearts that they are making a valuable contribution to the team and the organization.

> *What drives people the most is a sense of belonging and the feeling that they are playing an important part in the team's success.*

It is not always easy to come up with a monetary reward, especially when budgets are very tight and increases are not as generous as in past years. And yet sometimes, simple acts of appreciation can actually go a long way with your team. It involves listening carefully and paying attention throughout the year to find out more about each one of your team members as you plan for your rewards.

Here are a few ideas that have worked for me:

1. Bring in cookies or the person's favorite food. Even if you don't know how to bake, I'm sure you can afford to spend a few dollars to buy cookies from a bakery, or a specialty food that you know your team member enjoys.

2. Give a book on a topic in which you know he or she is interested. Or, give a book that can help them grow and improve their lives. This special gift can even create an excellent way to connect with your team on a more personal level as you discuss its contents.

3. Take them to lunch on your own dime. I understand that this can be a financial strain for you. But, when possible, and not only when it's an anniversary or a birthday, treat a team member to lunch. The time you spend together away from the work environment can create an opportunity for conversations that may not occur at work.

4. Recognize an individual's efforts and praise his or her work during a team meeting. Or, when you receive kudos for a job well done by one of your team members or superiors, share that with the bigger group and express your appreciation as well. Be mindful about public praise though, especially if the person involved doesn't like to be acknowledged openly.

5. Create special certificates of appreciation for a specific project for which you want to recognize the team. It can be as simple as printing these certificates on a regular printer at the office and presenting these during a team meeting.

6. Give the person a handwritten thank-you card. Email messages, or e-cards are good, too, but sometimes that handwritten card personally signed feels warmer and more effective.

7. Say a simple "Thank you" that comes from your heart. Be sure though that you give your thanks timely and sparingly. Saying, "Thank you" a week after an event won't have the same effect as recognizing good work right when it happens. Also, when you constantly say, "Thank you," it will lose its value after a while, causing your words to fall on deaf ears.

8. Invite your team over to your place for a get-together. Either a dinner or a late lunch can bring

the team together away from the work setting. You can get to know the real people beyond the physical body whom we sometimes don't get to meet because we're too caught up in the craziness of our daily work routine.

As much as appreciation is important to maintain the spirit and morale of the team, it's just as crucial to be careful about how and when appreciation is given. Keep in mind that not everyone has the same skills. So, you have to find an attribute in each one of your team members and praise him or her based on that attribute, noting the accomplishment that supports his or her strengths. When the team senses that you value one member more than the rest of the group, this can stir up controversy, jealousy, competitiveness and resentment amongst the group. As a result, your efforts of appreciation will backfire, and you will be seen as a leader who plays favorites.

H-E-A-*R*-T = Respect

How do you earn your team's respect? It's easy! Simply, respect them first. You can't expect your team to respect you as their leader if *you* lack courtesy and are rude.

Sometimes, it's easy to allow your ego to take over. Because you're the leader, you expect your team to conform to your ideas even if they may not be brilliant. Or, you presume your team will jump at your every request. But, that's not realistic. Your team members are as human as you are. They have similar feelings, fears, thoughts, problems and issues in life, as well as ideas that may be better than yours. If they do not support your ideas and share your own opinion, it's important for you to respect their input and take it seriously. Trying to understand where they are coming from will ensure you are not viewed as an opinionated leader. Instead, you will earn their respect. The team will see you as a leader who listens and values his or her team's input. Keep in mind, just because you are the leader you don't have to be the one with the ideas all the time.

I'm sure you agree that when there's mutual respect, work gets done faster, smoother and easier. Projects are finalized with accuracy, and the team feels engaged and part of the process.

In order to foster that respect, it's vital that you say what you mean, and mean what you say. Make sure you don't have a hidden agenda when you share information. If your team realizes that you're not being sincere or candid, they'll be able to see through it. You can then kiss that respect goodbye.

> *As a leader, it's vital that you say what you mean, and mean what you say.*

Make sure you keep your word when you promise something. Always deliver what you promise and deliver it on time. Value your team's work and respect any deadlines you receive from your team members. How do you expect them to care about the department's goals and project deadlines if you won't help them by keeping your own deadlines? Always keep in mind that actions speak louder than words. So, if you keep promising but never really delivering, eventually it will catch up with you. And, once again, you can kiss that respect goodbye.

> *If you keep promising but never really delivering, eventually it will catch up with you.*

Give the team timely updates on important information. If there's an error or something doesn't go as planned, let them know. They'll understand that you, too, are a human being and that you also make mistakes. They'll actually respect you even more for your candidness. Generally it takes years to earn a person's respect, but losing it can be instantaneous. So, do fess up when you mess up, and be sure to practice what you preach.

H-E-A-R- *T* = *T*rust

Another vital characteristic to have as a leader is trustworthiness. This goes hand in hand with the two characteristics we discussed earlier: honesty and respect. You can't be trusted if you're not honest and respectful toward others. One can't exist without the other two.

If you're not sincere with your team, they won't believe you. Instead, they'll wonder whether you're hiding information from them to suit your own agenda.

A perfect example is the boy in Aesop's fable. He cried wolf three times, each time expecting his friends to help him. You know how the story ends. The first two times, the villagers ran to help, only to find the boy laughing uncontrollably. The third time, when the boy cried wolf, no one bothered to come, even though this time the boy was telling the truth. Alas, the boy's sheep were eaten by the wolf.

The reality is that, you, as a leader, may not even get three chances. If you're caught lying even once, your team won't trust you. They'll doubt your promises and won't take you seriously. If you lie, say things that you don't mean, don't admit your mistakes, or withhold necessary information, eventually, everyone will think that you're full of hot air and not worthy of their respect.

Even if you can't deliver what they want, be honest about it. Tell them what you can do for them instead. The team needs to feel that you have their best interests in mind and that you're there for them. To help you build your relationship with your team, it's crucial that you keep your word and, most importantly, that you are truthful with your words.

Keep in mind an organization's rumor mill is very strong. And, usually, there's some truth to a rumor, albeit slightly exaggerated or tweaked. So, hiding behind the truth doesn't make it any better for you as a leader. Instead, the team will feel that you undermine their judgment and intelligence if you try to sugarcoat everything instead of addressing issues directly. Be straightforward and get to the point. I've heard too many leaders during my career beat around the bush as they try to justify their actions, coming up with reasons and explanations that make no sense. Avoid that pitfall. Trust and respect your team enough to share with them the real situation at hand. They will appreciate your honesty.

> *Trust and respect your team enough to share with them the real situation at hand.*

Just because you're a leader doesn't mean you can't be human and let your guard down once in a while.

Reaching deep into your heart will help you to be considerate, understanding and supportive of your team. Sugarcoating issues is not a good approach, because your team members are also professionals who see and hear things and can make their own judgments regardless of what you say. Be truthful and candid with whatever the situation. Do these things, and, before you know it, you'll have earned your team's trust. Your team and colleagues will value your input and look up to you as their leader.

POWER vs. *Heart* in Leadership

Chapter III

Who, What, When, and Why?

Power is of two kinds. One is obtained by the fear of punishment and the other by acts of love. Power based on love is a thousand times more effective and permanent then the one derived from fear of punishment.

–Mahatma Gandhi

Leadership is hard work—no doubt about it. At times, you may feel like giving up. Or, you may feel as if your team let you down. Sometimes, you may feel lonely at the top or, you may be challenged or put on the spot. That's why you have to be on your toes at all times, able to respond and meet your team's needs while letting go of your own.

When you help others develop professionally and grow in their careers, you will get more in return as a leader. Watching your team members grow in their roles will give you satisfaction and a sense of achievement. And, having a high-performing team reflects positively on your leadership skills. Their accomplishments are also your own. When your team completes a project successfully, this means that your goals are also being met. You'll be recognized as an effective leader. And, your own career may even take off. Before you know it, new opportunities will come your way.

The important point is to let go of your ego and pride along the way. As an effective leader, you have to be a good listener and keep an open mind when your team comes to you with suggestions or ideas. Just because you are the leader doesn't mean you're going to be right all the time. It's okay to make a mistake once in a while. And, it's okay to learn something new from your team members. You can't know it all. It's okay to ask for help when you can't do it all. You're not a superhero, even though at times you may want everyone to believe that you are.

And, just when you think you're getting this leadership thing down, finally figuring things out, you may be faced with a new situation that needs to be dealt with. Once again you'll find yourself in a state where you need to stop, listen to the problem carefully before coming to conclusions, and possibly learn something new and adapt accordingly. It's crucial that you let go of any disagreements, take a deep breath and forego any personal feelings. When you stop and really listen to the issue, you are able to reach deep into your soul to understand the situation better. In return, you are able to handle things with calmness and inner strength instead of letting your ego take over.

A few examples of such a situation could be an underperforming team member; a micromanaging boss of your own who questions your decisions and actions, putting you in an awkward situation with your team; an uncooperative colleague who stabs you in the back as he or she tries to raise his or her prestige; or, a very demanding stakeholder with whom you frequently disagree and yet need to play the political game with to ensure he or she is satisfied.

In facing these challenges, one key element is often ignored by those in leadership positions: the support and loyalty of those they lead. Remember, being a leader is an appointed position. However, gaining the respect of those you lead is earned, regardless of where you work and the position you hold.

I've always believed that the most important position in an organization is that of a receptionist, or the person who answers the phones. Why you may ask? Well, think about it for a second—the receptionist or the telephone operator is the very first person a potential customer, or an existing customer talks to when he or she contacts the company. If that receptionist is pleasant and service oriented, your customer will have a positive experience, giving them a positive impression of the company. And, ultimately, a satisfied customer will return and most probably recommend the company to others as well.

Now let's look at a different picture. If that receptionist or telephone operator is rude or doesn't make an effort to answer a question or help resolve the issue at hand, the customer will share his or her bad experience with another seven to ten people, spreading the word about his or her negative experience and saying what a bad company you have. Now, do you see why it's important for you, as a leader, to make sure you don't lose touch with front-line employees? Every single position in a company is important. And, as leaders, it is crucial to be able to connect with your people, talk to them, and get their input and suggestions, no matter what their level is. After all, front-line employees are the ones interacting with your customers every day. They are the ones dealing with the problems. You may think you know what the answers to most problems are, but when you connect with front-line staff and listen to what they have to say, you may be surprised to find out that you were completely off track. As you talk to the team, you may have one of those "aha" moments, realizing that there's more to the problem than you originally thought.

The lesson learned here is that every leader can learn from anyone on his or her team.

Getting the work done

As a leader, your job is to encourage the team and inspire them to get the work done with enthusiasm and zeal. You are also there to guide them in the right direction, focusing on their strengths and enabling them to grow even more in their position. How can you do that when you don't have a relationship of trust and loyalty with the team? This is where all of the five *H -E -A -R -T* elements play a major role in helping you accomplish your mission as a leader.

It's important to show genuine interest and eagerness to know more about your team, engaging them in decisions and asking for feedback.

There are areas you can focus on to help you achieve a level of trust and respect, as well as earn the loyalty of your team as you build a supportive environment that is unparalleled. Keep in mind that your approach for each one of these areas must first be filtered through your heart and humanized with emotion and understanding. Faking any of these elements will not get you far. Sincerity is key.

Who are they?

It's essential to make an effort to connect with your team and learn more about them and their families. How are their parents doing? Are there any siblings involved that may be the cause of stress for your employee? Do they have children? If yes, how they are doing? This doesn't mean that you become nosy or ask inappropriate personal questions. Rather, you should be aware of what's going on in their lives, especially as it may be affecting their performance.

You must also be careful that your interest is not phony and done just for the sake of showing interest. Instead, your attention must be genuine. Learning more about their lives will help you understand where they are coming from and how you can support them in order for them to succeed.

What makes them tick?

As a leader, it's also important to get to know your team—learn what they are passionate about and what makes each of them tick. Take the time to understand what energizes them and makes them want to go that extra mile, going above and beyond your expectations.

Do you know what makes your team truly content and happy? Do you sometimes feel as if your efforts are in vain? Take a step back and examine whether you actually understand your team and what they want.

Sometimes, we try to treat others the way we would want to be treated. But, that's not always the way to go. As the idiom says, "One man's meat is another man's poison." So, as you get to know your team on a deeper level, you'll be able to learn what their "meat" is instead of trying to make them happy by giving them your "meat," which could be poisoning them. The Golden Rule says, "Do unto others as you would have them do unto you." But, the platinum rule says, "Treat others in the way they like to be treated."

Why is it important to understand what makes your team happy? Simple! Because happy employees are satisfied, and as a result, they are more focused, productive, excited about their job and eager to come to work every day.

You may be asking "What's in it for me to go to all the effort of trying to figure out each of my team member's likes and dislikes?" By reaching out to your team, you will undoubtedly make them feel appreciated and valued. In return, they will feel happy; and, happy employees are pleasant to work with and eager to do what it takes to get the job done. A happy team is a cohesive team that works well together, as each member respects and helps the other. And, as a result, your work as a leader becomes a lot easier and simpler.

Just think for a second how chaotic it would be if you had to manage people's emotions and behaviors all day because of unhappiness and distrust amongst the team. As people point at each other, they can't focus their energy on their work. Instead, they focus on their negative feelings. You cannot be productive if throughout the day you are pulled in different directions to put out fires because your team is not performing up to par. Of course, let's not forget the humiliation this may cause you as their leader, since, ultimately, your team's performance (or lack thereof) reflects on you and your leadership skills.

> *Your team's performance (or lack thereof) reflects on you and your leadership skills.*

I know we touched on this earlier, but it's important enough to repeat it here: When you connect with your team on a more personal level and get more acquainted with their families, children, grandchildren, their hobbies and interests, you are able to understand them better as human beings and figure out what really drives them. You are then better equipped to address their needs and set your expectations based on their capabilities and aspirations. Try this approach, and before you know it, you will be able to reach out to your team and understand each other at a deeper level, soul to soul.

The more you get to know each other, the stronger and more profound your relationship becomes. And, the stronger the relationship, the better chance you have of building a solid foundation. A relationship built on a solid foundation has a better chance of surviving tough times. To help you build this strong foundation, you must continue to develop the five characteristics of the *H-E-A-R-T*: *H*umility, *E*quality, *A*ppreciation, *R*espect and *T*rust.

The end result of your efforts? Your team will be loyal to you and willing to take the plunge for you when things get tough in order to complete a project on time and within budget.

You're human too

We've talked about being able to acknowledge when you make a mistake or admit when you don't have all the answers. Self-deprecate when appropriate, but be sure you don't exaggerate. Though putting yourself down may make you appear human, my experience has been that your team may not always appreciate hearing their leader's shortcomings.

If you change your mind on a prior decision, or if you make a mistake, saying so and admitting you are at fault, or that you realize the direction in which you were originally headed needs to change, is actually a respectable approach that your team will appreciate. However, be sure you come clean with your team. Explain the reason you need to make the change instead of just telling them about the new direction you've decided to take.

It's also important to involve your team, hearing their input before you decide which route to take. This approach will ensure you get their buy-in, and, because of that, they'll be fully engaged in helping you make the change a success. On the contrary, if a change is forced on your team, you run the risk of losing your best performers. Even worse, they may continue to stick around, but will be demoralized. Eventually their productivity will be reduced, affecting customer service.

Do they know?

Communicate, communicate, communicate. The more you communicate, the better. This is an area in which most leaders fail. Don't assume your team knows what's going on. Or, even worse, don't leave them in the dark with what's happening on a project or deprive them of important updates. Of course, I'm not talking about information that may be classified as confidential and should not be shared. Instead, I'm referring to information that you may have heard at a meeting or heard from your leaders that your team could benefit from knowing as well.

You may think that holding on to information makes you powerful, yet the reality is that sharing knowledge benefits you. When you share, your team looks at you as a reliable resource and someone they can go to for answers.

It's important to ensure that your team is up to date on what is going on and why. Schedule regular team meetings, and don't cancel them. All too often, leaders tend to allow other meetings to bump their team meetings. Or, team meetings are cut short and are not productive.

When you cancel team meetings on a regular basis, you send an underlying message to your team that these meetings and your team are not your priority. As a result, team members lose their respect and trust in you as their leader. Because of that, their loyalty diminishes, and consequently, cooperation and teamwork suffers.

To avoid all of the above pitfalls, make sure you communicate regularly; prepare for your team meetings and come organized with a well-thought-out agenda. Cancel a meeting only if it is absolutely necessary, but be sure to reschedule.

Keep on learning

Encourage a learning culture within your team. Be a role model by starting with yourself. Lifelong learning is not a 9 to 5 situation; it's about how you absorb new experiences, whether at work, through community service, training courses, assignments, reading, or travel. It's a reciprocal process: Employers provide opportunities to learn and grow, but employees also need to engage in activities outside of work.

It's okay to socialize

Most leaders are afraid to socialize with their subordinates. As we discussed in earlier sections, it's okay to get together with your team outside of the work environment. This is how you build a stronger relationship. However, take particular care, as a leader, to never be seen as having favorites, which may occur through social activities. If you are going to socialize, make sure you're engaging the entire team. And remember, it's important that you limit your alcohol intake during such activities. You need to maintain your composure at all times. Lead by example!

Give appropriate and timely feedback

Give regular feedback on performance. Make sure you don't wait for performance review time to give input on how your people are doing. Be open and honest without being hurtful. Just because you are the leader, doesn't mean you have the right to humiliate or put someone down for a possible mistake or mishap.

Unfortunately, all too often, performance reviews are based on one or two issues that happen closer to the time a performance review is written instead of taking into consideration all the work a person has accomplished throughout the entire year. If a person made one mistake and yet excelled in ten other areas, don't focus on the mistake. Instead, first praise him or her on the excellent outcomes and then mention how his or her performance could be even better next time if he or she paid attention to the area of the mistake.

Acknowledge and recognize superior performance when you see it. Most importantly, give specific examples about activities you are rating as needing improvement or those done exceptionally well. This helps make the connection and keeps the performance feedback real.

> *Acknowledge and recognize superior performance when you see it.*

Micromanaging doesn't work

Avoid micromanaging your team. As they gain work experience and grow in their positions, keep their interest by giving them increased responsibility and leadership opportunities. You will be doing your good performers a disservice if you don't help them learn more and start taking on higher-level work. This will free you up to take on other things, too, as you grow in your position.

The fundamental skill you must have as a leader is to be able to help your team members believe in themselves and try to build their confidence. "How," you may ask, "do I do that?" Here's a simple way: let them make their own mistakes (to a certain extent). Instead of giving them the answer, show them where to go for it, or explain the details involved and allow them to work things out. Ultimately, you are responsible for your team's work—I realize that. But, there does need to be room for growth and learning.

Sometimes, it may be scary and intimidating as they challenge you with their questions or the increased expectation they have of you as their leader. Park your ego and share the leadership, as appropriate.

You must ensure you do not lose your edge by continuing to learn and increasing your own knowledge of your industry and position.

> *Park your ego and share the leadership, as appropriate.*

Back your team

There are leaders who tend to backpedal when things don't go as planned. They go as far as denying what they originally directed the team to do. It's funny how quickly some leaders develop a preferred memory loss of what happened just to cover their own behind.

I understand things can't always be black and white, or have a straight yes or no answer. Nevertheless, no matter what the outcome is, a strong leader will always stand behind his or her decision, explaining the reasons for the decision without wavering at the first obstacle or challenge. This is the first step toward building that trust with the team we've talked about throughout this book.

At times leaders are busy trying to cover their own skin when a problem arises as a result of a mistake their team made. Remember, when your team makes mistakes, you are responsible for their performance, as much as you take the glory when they do a good job. So stand behind your team during times of difficulty.

If the team gets caught up in organizational politics and is in trouble, don't abandon them in an attempt to save yourself. Unless the mistake involves illegal or other unethical behaviors, there is no reason for you to allow your own superiors to mistreat your team. This is the time when you show your team they can really rely on you to be there for them.

If you can't stand behind your team members, then you are not worthy to be their leader—and you'll certainly not gain much of their trust or respect any time soon. On the contrary, it is in situations like this that team members begin to evaluate and figure out whether their leader is authentic or just gives lip service.

POWER vs. *Heart* in Leadership

CHAPTER IV

Your True Self

When you are content to be simply yourself and don't compare or compete, everybody will respect you.
—Lao Tzu

When was the last time you doubted yourself and questioned your leadership skills? Maybe someone's words had an adverse effect on you and you felt incompetent or ineffective as a leader. Maybe you even wondered if you were worthy of the position you held. Or, the other way around, maybe you wondered why you were staying in the position you were in instead of moving on and up.

Sometimes you may have felt down and frustrated as a leader, asking yourself, "Why do I even bother to work as hard as I do, trying to improve things when no one seems to listen or understand my point of view? Why do I care so much?" I'm sure you've also been told by other colleagues to "just go with the flow; be flexible and don't make any waves," even though your point of view was valid and could bring value to the company.

If you have had any of the above thoughts, feelings and/or experiences, trust me, you're not alone. Having these thoughts and emotions is a sign that you are eager to grow as a leader and that you really care about your job. But, in searching for answers, you may be challenged by your superiors who may be neither supportive nor encouraging. It's during such times when, instead of looking outward for answers, all you need to do is first look within yourself, understanding who you are as a leader and what your values are.

You must first believe in yourself in order to exude that leadership confidence (and I'm not referring to an egotistical superiority complex here). When you're confident in your own abilities as a leader, it will be apparent in your actions and behavior. You'll be more in tune with your True Self and will start trusting your intuition and gut feelings as you make decisions. Your team will feel your positive energy and you will start to attract similar people to your group.

Knowing your True Self

You may be wondering, "What is my True Self?" There aren't words to fully describe your True Self. But, I will try my best to explain. Your True Self comes with no preconceptions or judgments of others. Your True Self is accepting and forgiving. It's your pure and unconditioned soul, which, as you grew up and got caught up with society's expectations as well as your personal life experiences, possibly got buried where it became harder and harder for you to reach.

Your True Self is that soft inner voice that guides you when everything else fails. It knows what you need to do even though your logic may tell you otherwise. You just know when something is not right because you get a bad feeling when you think about it. That's when you need to rely on your gut and trust what you feel.

How do you allow your True Self to resurface so that you can re-establish a connection? The simplest way is for you to sit quietly by yourself, close your eyes, take a few deep breaths and focus on the situation at hand. Let your natural instinct guide you as you ask for guidance within. That's when you are able to really connect with your True Self—your soul, where you can find inner peace and gain clarity of your questions. To reach deep inside your being, don't allow any distractions to interfere with your special time. When what you are thinking of doing does not evoke peace and satisfaction in your gut, then I would recommend that you think again before taking action.

> *Your True Self is that soft inner voice that guides you when everything else fails.*

The good part is that you can tap into your True Self as often as you want, and wherever you are. Commit to taking time each day, sit quietly by yourself and focus within your inner being. Daily practice of meditation definitely helps you make this connection faster.

You may be wondering what all of this has to do with leadership. All of this goes back to the *H -E -A -R -T* of the matter. Having a pure soul and good intentions when dealing with people is the key to a leader's success. Your True Self will help you get rid of misconceptions, preconceptions, resentments and any judgments you may have of those you work with. Once you connect to your True Self, your entire perception and expectation of others will change, because now you will be focusing on your behaviors and how you can become a better person and a blessing to those you lead rather than on how you can control, manipulate or change them.

You may also be asking, "How would I know if I am connected to my True Self and that it's not just my ego talking to me? There is no easy answer to this question other than you'll know when you have made that shift.

When you make that connection with your True Self, you begin to see those around you differently. Your heart becomes more open and accepting. You are able to understand where others

> *When you make that connection with your True Self, you begin to see those around you differently.*

are coming from. Instead of fighting the situation or wanting to be right all the time, you try to find solutions that help others rather than feed your ego. You bond with your team at a deeper level instead of simply being a leader who tells them what to do. It's almost as if you can feel what they feel and be one with their energy field.

The more you strengthen your intuition, the more you feel connected with your soul, your True Self. As you cultivate your True Self, your intuition, gut feeling—or whatever you may call it—also becomes stronger. Even though you may not be able to make any sense of it at the time, you are then able to trust your judgment, or that hunch you have about certain situations or people.

When you rely on your five senses alone, your interactions with your team remain superficial and unsatisfactory for both parties. However, the more you develop your sixth sense (which is also called your third eye), certain emotions surface that you may not have felt before. The more connected you are, the more you start seeing or feeling things that you didn't before. For example, a colleague pays you a compliment, yet you can sense that he or she is not being genuine; you can tell that he or she just has a hidden agenda; your manager may be all smiles telling you all is fine, yet you can sense that he or she is not being honest with you; a staff member may be going about his or her day, but you can feel from their energy that something is bothering them. Or, you may know something is not right when you are about to take action and you have that uncomfortable feeling that's nagging you. Yet, you may not listen to that little voice telling you that's not the way to go. I have learned not to ignore that voice, no matter how tiny it is.

The power within

Knowing how to treat another human being with dignity, respect and kindness is a virtue owned by someone who is connected with his or her higher existence at all times. This person realizes that no matter his or her position or standing in life, it's important to value all human beings, leading by serving and mentoring his or her team to success.

Undoubtedly, there will be times when things get tough. You will be faced with obstacles and your patience will be tested. You may have to lead a team that needs more attention, nurturing and support than a normal team would need. How will you act in this situation? Will you be understanding and patient? Or, are you going to rebuke your team's needs? Your true colors will come through when you're under pressure.

When choosing fruit, we tend to pick the ones that appear fresh and free of any smudges. But sometimes, when we cut into the fruit, we find that it has started rotting right at its core. Or, it doesn't taste as good as we thought it might despite how it looked. The same is true with people.

Acting or pretending to be nice on the outside when things are going well is easy. However, if your heart—your "core"—is not pure, caring and loving toward people, eventually your true colors will show. When a stressful situation arises, what's truly inside you will come out. If you have anger, resentment and dislike toward your team, it will be very hard to be kind and understanding. Ultimately, your anger, resentment and dislike will spill over. However, if your heart is pure and loving toward your team, even in the toughest situations you will be able to show how much you care and understand where they are coming from, being as supportive as possible.

Kindness doesn't mean weakness

Going down memory lane, I remember my very first manager. She was an older lady who cared about her staff and was always there to help and support. She never hesitated to step in and explain a process in detail to ensure we knew how to approach a situation. And, if things needed to be corrected, she approached the issue in such a way so as not to offend anyone or point any fingers. Though she was kind and caring, she sure was demanding, and her expectations were high. She was incredibly sharp, always trying to learn new things to maintain her edge. She gave me my first glimpse of what it meant to be a true leader. Even though there were a number of younger managers who reported to her and many more who worked with her on various projects, everyone respected and looked up to her as a leader.

Another manager I had the pleasure of working for was a brilliant man. He too was demanding with very high standards. But, at the same time, he was tenderhearted when it came to the human aspect of things. He knew how to make his people feel appreciated and supported. I learned from him, and he learned from me at different levels. He was a leader who was more interested in helping to solve an issue rather than trying to figure out whom to blame in the event of an error.

He was a leader comfortable in his own skin without the need to exercise any power, for his power came from his heart. Everyone liked him and was always willing and ready to help him with anything he needed. He treated everyone the same, from the office cleaners to the telephone operators and receptionists, all the way up to his managers and directors. He viewed every single one of his team members as equals and respected them as human beings.

Watch that mouth

I would like to stress here, once again, the importance of being genuine and sincere with your words. Sometimes, your words can damage a relationship if you come across as disingenuous. For example, don't compliment someone simply for the sake of it or because you feel obligated to do so.

One way to be genuine with your words is to find something that you do like about a person and focus on that when you give your compliment. This will ensure you come across as a sincere person. For example, if you don't like the dress a colleague is wearing but you truly love the color of the dress, why not just say that? "I love that color!" Otherwise, keeping your mouth shut is better than being dishonest.

Walking around with a chip on your shoulder or with a negative attitude will very quickly rub off on those around you. Your energy will have a ripple effect. And, before you know it, a dark cloud will loom over the entire team. If you are not aware of your own words and actions, you will be wondering why people are acting the way they are.

The bottom line is, if there's nothing positive or kind you can say about a person or a situation, just don't say anything at all. Once you say something, you can't take it back—the harm is done! In these situations, silence **is** golden.

Take heart

Leading from your heart instead of using your position power means that, as a leader, you don't try to manipulate, pressure or possibly even bully people into doing what you want. Leading from your heart means listening to your True Self and not allowing all the noise around you or the pressure from others to change your heart. As I mentioned earlier, dig deep inside and let your True Self guide you, because your intuition (or your soul, your gut feeling) is connected to your True Self; and your True Self is rarely wrong. That's why a leader who is genuine and open with his or her team makes a huge positive impact on the team and the workplace as a whole.

As you start to understand the difference between leading with your heart instead of using your position power, you will notice that it may get harder for you as a leader. Those around you may not appreciate your approach and may start making judgments based on their preconceptions of how a leader should behave. Your own manager or peers may not understand your leadership style and may condemn you for not being tough enough with your team. Remain true to your True Self and trust that you are doing the right thing.

Unfortunately, all too often, leaders believe that it's necessary for them to be hard-core and show a tough image to their subordinates. The reality is that you need to have a balance. As a leader, yes, it's important to maintain that leadership image, but your team must also see your human side. If you are constantly portraying a façade that is emotionless, cold, and curt, your relationship with the team will suffer, and, eventually, it will impact workflow and production. The more you connect with the group, the more you will open up to the team, allowing them to feel safe to share their ideas and opinions with you. Consequently the work environment will become warmer and healthier, with increased productivity and better results overall.

> *As a leader, yes, it's important to maintain that leadership image, but your team must also see your human side.*

Enough with the sugarcoating

Another area that leaders must be mindful of is the tendency to constantly toot the company's horn, trying to make everything sound great when, in reality, things may not be as good. Some managers continuously act as cheerleaders, trying to be enthusiastic and energized in an effort to convince their team that every decision made by senior leaders is just excellent and for the employees' own benefit! In reality, this type of leadership style has its drawbacks. When you always operate under the Pollyanna syndrome, you must remember that those who report to you are not blind.

> *It is important for leaders to be authentic and true to themselves and their teams.*

No matter how much you may cheer as a leader, your team can see and feel certain things. If you, as their leader, do not address the bad with the good, you will lose your team's trust. Of course, it's expected that leaders would be supportive of their own leaders' goals and objectives—that's totally understandable. Nonetheless, it is also important for leaders to be authentic and true to themselves and their teams.

Be true to yourself

I've always been a supporter of the fact that, as a leader, one must encourage, inspire, and care about one's team at all times. Conversely, I also believe that being fake in order to try and convince your team about an issue or a decision that you don't believe in is actually like lying to yourself.

I can't stress enough the importance of being true to yourself first before you can even start helping your team deal with their issues. You can't really influence and lead a team to success if you are not true to your own beliefs first.

I understand that, at times, an organization makes decisions that, as a leader you must support, even if these decisions go against your grain. If that's the case, it's okay to let your team know that the decision was an organizational one, and explain that whether you agree with the decision or not, it's important that you support the company's direction. At the same time, look within yourself to see what about this decision you can genuinely work with and how you can positively influence your team to accept whatever the decision at hand may be and move forward.

Being able to admit that you may not always agree with decisions, but that some things are also imposed on you as a leader, brings a sense of reality to the situation. Your team recognizes that you are human too, with your own feelings and thoughts, and not a programmed robot that embraces any decision that comes from the top without questioning its validity.

If you're honest with the team and explain that, even though things don't seem to be what we would have liked, we still need to support and get the job done to move things along, your team will respect you for your honesty and follow you no matter where you take them.

Being true to yourself also brings a sense of peace within you. You have the comfort of knowing that even though you may not always agree with the company's decisions, you are able to respect your own thoughts and feelings about the decision, address these with your team and ask for their help and support.

When to use your power

As you've read throughout this book, leading with your heart is vital to your success and the well-being of your team. That doesn't mean that there won't be times when you have to use the position power you have to make certain executive decisions. One of the worst characteristics in a leader is indecisiveness. You must be able to take accountability and make the necessary tough decisions. You will have to deliver bad news at times. You may need to consult with an employee who is not performing, or, a task every leader dreads, you may have to tell someone that he or she is being let go.

All of the aforementioned are duties that go hand in hand with being a leader. Yet, this doesn't mean that, as you work through these issues, your position power should take over your heart.

I'm not implying that power is not important. What I am trying to convey is that it all depends how this power is used. I've seen over and over again leaders who let their position power go to their head, and they start looking down at people, even those with whom they used to work as colleagues prior to their promotion. All of a sudden, they develop an attitude, an image that creates a distance between them and their former peers, sending a negative message to them that, "I am the leader, so you need to respect me and heed me…or else." I realize that it can be an uncomfortable situation when you are promoted and find yourself leading your peers. The key is to make that transition gracefully, without leaving "dead bodies" behind and tarnishing your relationships. Keep in mind that you may need your ex-peers—should they become part of your team—to do the job for you, and do it right.

Even in the toughest situations, if you reach down deep within your soul and feel your heart, you will know the right thing to say or do. You will know again by the peacefulness or turbulence you will feel as

> *If you reach down deep within your soul and feel your heart, you will know what the right thing to say or do is.*

you think about each approach. It's important to take your time and think through things carefully before you jump to a decision and come to conclusions. Generally, that first instinctive reaction you have is the right one. Trust it and listen to your inner voice.

True meaning of power

When you think of a powerful person, who comes to mind? A president of a country? A chief executive officer, president, or vice president of a company? A politician? Maybe a doctor or professor? How about a famous actor or actress? Or a billionaire?

It's true that all of these people, because of their high-level executive positions and specialties, or their wealth, have a lot of power they can exercise. Obviously, they can say yea or nay to any situation when they are responsible for making a decision. They also have the power to decide whether to fire or hire people, regardless of the reason or fairness of the situation, just because they hold that position.

These are some of the reasons that those who work for powerful executives are more than eager to satisfy the executives' wants and needs. They don't want to be on their executives' black list and possibly find themselves out of a job.

Sure, you'll almost always get what you want when you need it and how you want it because of your position power. But, is that truly the kind of power you want? People who smile at your face and say what you want to hear, but gossip and shred you to pieces behind your back? People who hate your guts and are happy to see you fail?

Position power, if not coupled with the humane characteristics, is not one to be coveted. People fear your next step or decision—not knowing how it may affect their livelihood.

The reality is that true power doesn't come with a position. Here's what I mean. If you are a leader who treats people fairly and connects with them at the heart level, you'll have flocks of people following you. They'll have confidence in you and have no problem taking your directives. They'll want to please you not because of your position power, but because they genuinely care and want to help you out. Why? Because they respect you as a person and know you will deliver what you promise, and you'll be there for them when they need you as well. And, most importantly, they know that you won't take the credit for the work they've done.

So, we're back to what I have shared earlier in this book. The most important characteristic of a leader is not his or her education, position or money. A leader, in the true sense of the word, is someone who is always there for his or her team, colleagues and coworkers, no matter what. He or she can roll up his or her sleeves and help his or her team when they need the support, just like he or she would for family members and friends. A leader has his or her team's best interest in mind, giving them the credit they deserve.

Who can be a leader?

"Are leaders born or made?" Ah, the infamous question that has been asked for ages. There are numerous interpretations on this subject. Some say leaders are born, while others insist that leaders can be made.

> *What differentiates a regular leader from a noble leader is his or her gift or ability to treat people from the heart...*

My belief has always been that certain leadership skills can be taught and developed with years of practice and experience. But, what differentiates a regular leader from a noble leader is his or her gift or ability to treat people from the heart, refusing to abuse the power that comes with his or her position.

A person can have the people skills required to lead, but no matter how much training and experience he or she gets, these are intangible skills that need to be expressed with sincerity, coming from the heart.

I believe that what one can be taught is limited in nature. A true leader is born with that inner ability that shines through, and people are drawn to this person from the inside out. Caring for people cannot be forced just because someone says that's how leaders should act. You can't teach someone to be genuinely caring, loving and sympathetic. These qualities have to come from the heart. He or she has to be authentic with an innate knowledge of how to treat people, and help them grow without making them feel incompetent because of potential limitations or drawbacks they may have as they try to learn.

If your interactions are unnatural because it's expected of you as a leader, you may be able to wing it for a while. But, if your intentions are not honest, sincere, and do not come from your heart, eventually, your team will catch on to you.

To be a leader in every sense of the word, you must be a people person. You need to understand what needs to be done in tough situations without feeling squeamish about making decisions. Too often, leaders are intimidated—they don't want to be the one to make a decision in case things don't work out. Their answers are vague and can be interpreted in various ways.

Sometimes their words sound more like a response that one gets from an attorney (no offense to all the attorneys out there), "Yes, but … and maybe… or not." And, it is up to the listener to make his or her own assumptions. After you've had a conversation with these types of leaders, you end up wondering what he or she just said and whether the answer was a yes or a no.

You've got it or you don't

I am a strong advocate for the idea that as far as true leadership skills go, you've either got it or you don't. Unless you truly want to change your behavior and dig deep within yourself and work through your personal issues, you will not be able to gain the trust and respect of your followers, especially if you lie, change your mind all the time and fail to back them up if things don't work out as planned. These are some of the reasons there are so many mediocre leaders out there who think that their role is to be on the lookout for errors. As soon as they catch someone with a mistake, they're ready to discipline the person. And worse yet, they're even ready to fire him or her because he or she had the guts to stand up for him or herself and disagree with the leader on certain topics. Though there are laws and policies to protect employees against retaliation and whistleblowers, throughout my entire career I've not seen anyone survive for long if they said something that didn't sit well with senior leadership.

A true leader is someone who supports his or her team members, allowing them to grow and flourish into higher and better positions, without feeling any intimidation or remorse. A leader focuses on each employee's strengths instead of his or her weaknesses. Everyone is born with different gifts. We can't expect the same results from every single team member because everyone is unique with a different personality and varying needs. Let's take as an example a garden that has different flowers growing in it. Not all of them need the same amount of watering or care. A cactus can survive with minimal water, yet a rose or a daisy will need greater care. These flowers all look different, but they all adorn your garden and bring it together as a whole. The same applies to your team members. They all have different strengths, varying needs and requirements for care, but when you bring them together, they make up a strong team, each one bringing a skill the other doesn't have. That's why it's important to identify the strengths each team member has, playing to those strengths to ensure you're using your team to their fullest potential.

> *A leader focuses on each employee's strengths instead of his or her weaknesses.*

POWER vs. *Heart* in Leadership

CHAPTER V

Getting There

The measure of a man is what he does with power.
—Plato

All too often, leaders who reach a certain level in their careers look down at those who haven't made it through the ranks, quickly forgetting that they weren't always the top honchos either.

In cases where, for various reasons, leaders who join the company at a leadership level without having to work themselves up the ranks, seldom understand what it means to have to climb that ladder. And even sadder, lower-level administrative and clerical positions are not appreciated and valued properly as often as they should be, nor are these employees generally considered for promotions. In either case, leaders who move up through the ranks tend to be egocentric and unsympathetic toward all the hard work that has to be done by those on the front lines who are the lifeline of any organization.

As leaders, their position power blinds them, giving them a sense of entitlement. Egos start to grow, and eventually they treat their team members as their puppets. Selfish leaders want what they want, when they want it, and don't consider how much work and effort the team has to put in to make things happen. Worst of all, they don't listen to any possible issues and risks that their team may share with them. As a result, these leaders make decisions that eventually evolve into problems, requiring countless hours of work and energy to reverse and correct those problems. If they had simply paid attention to what their team was sharing originally, they could have possibly avoided all of the trouble, unnecessary expenses and long work hours.

Now let's look at the other side of the coin. Leaders who appreciate all the work that goes into the front-line jobs understand the value these employees bring to the company. They know that as much as leaders are important to a company's success, front-line employees who carry out the daily work are equally important, if not more. As a result, such leaders become servant leaders, supporting and engaging their teams before making decisions that can have major effects on the company.

> *As much as leaders are important to a company's success, front-line employees are equally important..*

Helping hands

Would you rather be a leader who is understanding, patient, helpful, and inspiring? Or, would you want to be a leader whom everyone views as a tyrant and whom everyone fears, trying to avoid you at all costs? I sure hope your choice was not the latter. Because the entire essence of this book is that power is not what makes things work. Being pushy and bossy won't get you too far. It's the heart of the matter that allows people to connect and learn from each other. Kindness, compassion and plain humanity toward each other are the values that work regardless of rank or stature in an organization, or society for that matter. Show some kindness, appreciation, caring and understanding and watch as great things happen, not only in your career but your personal world as well.

Always remember that it takes just one leader to believe in a person and be that helping hand. When you believe in someone and allow that person to take on more challenging opportunities in order to learn and grow in his or her career, you're not only displaying your own leadership talents, but you're also making an amazing change in a person's life.

How would you feel if all you heard during the day was nothing but putdowns? That you were not smart enough, or fast enough, or didn't have the ability to communicate well, or influence others, etc. Just think about it—nothing but constant negativity coming your way. Would that make you want to do more for this leader, or would you just be even more unmotivated and not care any longer?

If you believe that, as a leader, you should focus on a person's weaknesses and limitations and constantly point these out to the person with the hope that he or she will become more aware of his or her performance in these areas and eventually grow, you are very sorely mistaken and should not be in that position. Negative feedback and constant criticisms don't work. On the contrary, all the negative energy the employee receives at work lingers and follows him or her home, affecting his or her family and creating a vicious cycle. Now, this person starts internalizing your negative feedback, and all he or she can hear in his or her head is, "I can't do anything right. I am stupid. I am useless. I am not good enough." Undoubtedly, this person's productivity will suffer, which will ultimately affect your team's work.

Even though you are the leader of your team, you, too, have your own leader to whom you have to answer. If you are self-employed, you still have to answer to your clients. There is always someone we have to answer to. And, most likely, you have faced some of the issues I've shared throughout this book with your own leaders or clients.

One of the best practices for you as a leader is to listen to your heart and remember your own experience when your boss gave you negative feedback. Or, remember the time when one client was rude and unappreciative of your work. I'm sure being at the receiving end of these comments and/or behaviors was not pleasant.

The bottom line is that if you keep feeding yourself negative thoughts, eventually your brain will believe you and start thinking that you are useless and can't do anything right. Your confidence, along with your energy and enthusiasm, will be buried forever, your True Self will suffer, and you will become resentful and bitter with those around you. However, if you focus on your positive attributes and on what you can do well, feeding affirmations to your brain throughout the day, you'll definitely feel better. Subconsciously, your confidence will increase, and you'll want to take on more challenges and achieve more.

Just as it takes one person to help motivate a person, it takes just one rotten leader to shut down a person, leaving him or her feeling useless and incapable. Most employees come to work with the desire to succeed. When they are faced with negativity, constant putdowns and no encouragement from their leader, no matter how much they want to do well, their True Self— their soul—wants to do good and wants to learn and grow, the negative energy wins.

This reminds me of an old Native American story about a good wolf and a bad wolf that live inside each of us. These two wolves are constantly engaged in a fierce battle. The good wolf portrays the love, compassion, courage, honesty, and every other good virtue we have as human beings. The bad wolf represents anger, hatred, jealousy, envy, greed, and all other evils we are capable of. The question is, "Which wolf gets to win?" And the answer is, "The one we feed more."

The moral of the story is that if we constantly focus on the bad things or the weaknesses of the team and ignore what they are doing well, eventually we'll allow the bad wolf to get stronger and devour the good wolf, leaving us with nothing to work with but demoralized employees. If you continue in this type of negative leadership mode, the workplace will very quickly become stressful, full of angst, and you'll probably experience constant employee turnover. This same notion applies at school with teachers, at home with parents, and with friends.

Now, let's reverse this scenario:

As a leader, you can encourage your team member by giving him or her the opportunity to show the skills he or she possesses. I realize that by doing this, you are putting your own reputation on the line. However, at the same time, because you're giving a person the chance to learn and move up, as you see this person grow, you'll get more out of the experience than the actual person you're supporting.

Think back when you were trying to move up in your career. Who was that one person who stood behind you at all times and believed in you, being that helping hand you needed? Wasn't it that one leader who knew there was more in you than the rest of the people thought you had?

It's easy to promote and support someone who is already a great employee. But, it takes effort and patience to encourage and help the person who needs it the most. Yes, this person may be a little slow to catch on, or not as brilliant as the rest of the world would have expected, but, when a person is putting in 100 percent, that's what a leader must appreciate the most. Because, that shows your own ability to support and help grow the level of a person when the rest of the world has given up on him or her. That's when a helping hand comes into play.

It'll take time and a lot of energy to keep guiding and motivating the employee who may not be as far along in his or her set of skills. And, there will be times when those around you will make you doubt your efforts by saying that you're wasting your time. They'll try to drag you down. But, it's at times like these when you must listen to your gut feeling and trust your ability to identify a good person when you see one.

Is the view better at the top?

Generally, the higher one rises up the corporate ladder, the broader and brighter the view gets at the top. You get better fringe benefits and the pay definitely increases, which is something we all welcome. Also, your office likely gets bigger, with fancier furniture, too. But, all of these added benefits undoubtedly come with increased responsibilities and difficult decision-making accountabilities.

A while back, a friend and I were discussing whether top-level executives worked harder than those lower-level leaders and employees. The response my friend gave me made an impression on me, and is one that I'll always remember. My friend, who happens to be a high-level executive, shared that the view may be better at the top, but the work itself doesn't increase, it just becomes a different type of work. Instead of concentrating on the daily details, the focus now is on the broader/bigger picture. Possibly there are more meetings to attend, and definitely there is a need to be more adept at dealing with organizational politics. Nonetheless, regardless of the leader's rank, the key to success for those at the top is the same as for those who are halfway to the top or at the bottom of the totem pole. Without wavering, the success of all leaders is connected to having a supportive and skillful team—a team who is loyal and trustworthy and who can undertake an assignment or a project

> *When the team is effective, it's a direct indication of how efficient their leader is.*

and successfully bring it to fruition. When the team is effective, it's a direct indication of how efficient their leader is in his or her role.

I'm fine where I am

One of the lessons I've learned throughout my career is that not everyone wants to reach the top of the pyramid. Not everyone is competitive or zealous to climb that ladder to reach the top and breathe the air from the executive level. Certain people are satisfied just doing what they do throughout their careers and leading their lives out of the fast lane. Personally, I've had several colleagues who have been clerks when they started, and, 20 years later, they were still at that same position and level. When I asked them why they never applied for a higher position with better pay, their simple response was, "I'm fine where I am; I don't need the politics, the headaches and the added responsibilities that come with a higher position." For me, this was an eye opener. I didn't realize that someone wouldn't want to learn more and get to the next level. In my opinion, that was natural progression you made as years went by. You learned, and then you got better at what you did; and eventually your superiors recognized you for your hard work. A promotion and a raise came your way until you reached the top level or the level you desired in your career.

One of the major errors made by organizations is that they promote a team member who is not fit to be a leader or may not be ready to take on that role. As a result, this person fails as a leader as he or she reaches his or her own incompetency. Not only is this person unhappy, but he or she makes everyone around him or her crazy and unhappy as well—especially his or her direct reports who have to follow his or her lead.

As a leader, it's important that you observe and understand your team. You need to realize that some of your people will be more ambitious than others. Some will want to climb up through the leadership ranks. Some will even want to push you out the door to get your job. And, yet others will just want to come in to work, put it their 8-hour day and go home without worrying about what goes on at the top of the chain. Once we realize that not everyone can or wants to be a superstar on a team, we can then learn to value and appreciate team members who are happy to be where they are and do their job day in and day out as best as they can.

Chapter VI

No Followers, No Leader

I suppose leadership at one time meant muscles; but today it means getting along with people.
—Mahatma Gandhi

Let's think about this for a moment. Who would you be leading if no one wanted to follow you, if no one trusted you or respected you as his or her leader? Who would you be leading if no one valued your opinion or believed in you? You would definitely not be a leader in my book, even if people followed you out of fear or just because you had the title and the position power.

Don't be too quick to dismiss your team's feelings or expectations of you as their leader. Your team is the reason you are called a leader, not because of the position you hold. Like my son once naively asked me on Mother's Day, "Mom, if it weren't for me, you wouldn't be a mom, would you?" So, I'll ask you the same question as a leader: If it weren't for your team, you wouldn't be considered a leader, would you?

The bottom line is this: If, as a human being, you are connected to your soul, your True Self, and you look out for what's best for people, becoming a blessing to them, showing your love for who they are and appreciating what they do, you will effortlessly attract a crowd who will want to follow your leadership, no matter what your position or title. Be honest, be transparent, be candid and be sincere with your team.

> *Be honest, be transparent, be candid and be sincere with your team.*

Avoid having a hidden agenda or putting on a façade with a poker face. It's good for your team to know that you, too, are human with feelings, and that you, too, have to abide by certain decisions made by your leaders, even though you may not always agree with those decisions.

Think twice before you try to sell your ideas or impose changes you want to implement just because you think these ideas or changes are the right things to do.

Do you really want to know what changes need to be made and what the real issues are at work? Then, start paying close attention and listen to any concerns your team may be sharing with you. If you ignore the red flags they may be sending you directly or indirectly, you're eventually destined to fail. Any changes you implement won't be effective if your team doesn't buy into them. The sad reality is that, most likely, they will be unhappy, but they'll keep quiet and go along with your ideas, because you do have that position power, and everyone is afraid of losing a job. But, if they continue to be unhappy, eventually, you'll lose all of your hard workers, leaving behind your weakest links.

New or old?

Leaders who are new to the company tend to surround themselves with their own new crew when they come on board instead of promoting the existing staff who have been with the company for years and have proven themselves to be worthy. One of the reasons for that is for them to feel secure and supported by the people they hire. "We need new blood;" "We need fresh minds;" "We need a new approach;" "Just because we've done it that way before doesn't mean it's the right way;" etc. Because of this mentality, leaders have a tendency to hire people from the outside.

Don't get me wrong, I recognize the benefit of having "new bodies." The hope is that they'll be the source of new energy and exciting ideas. Of course, the fact that their pay will usually be less than a long-term employee's has a role to play. But, "new blood" doesn't always mean better ideas. It may just mean repeating an error or going back to a path that has proven wrong in years past.

It's important for leaders to appreciate these long-term employees and not undermine or write off the benefits and advantages they bring. The involvement of the long-term employees over the years, along with their experience, knowledge, and history with the company, is priceless. As a leader, it pays to value the input of team members who have had the opportunity to experience a problem firsthand instead of repeating the same mistakes. Why try to fix something that's not broken if it will only create yet another problem that was already addressed and fixed years ago? Or, even worse, why revert to old standards, when the current ones have evolved over the years based on prior efforts and experiences? Sometimes "new blood" is just that—new blood that needs to prove him or herself, making the same mistakes all over again.

I realize that no one is irreplaceable, and I have been reminded of it many times throughout my career. Yet, a lot of leaders don't take into consideration the fact that replacing a seasoned professional cannot happen overnight. You'll need to put in a lot of time, effort and energy to train someone new in order to get them up to speed, let alone bring them to the level where they can learn the history and background of what's what in a given organization and be able to ask the right questions at the right time.

And, here's a hint: if you keep your same old attitude with your employees, though your newly hired employee may eventually get to the level of a seasoned employee and learn the business, ultimately he or she will leave you, too. And, the cycle will start all over again.

Each time you have to start training a new employee, it takes you back a few steps and affects productivity. A constant turnover in staff also deflates the existing team and ruins morale. The workplace shouldn't be a place where you go to simply get a paycheck. It needs to be a place where you go to add value to the company, grow as a professional, and enjoy yourself while you work. Doing what you do with pride and confidence!

> *Each time you have to start training a new employee, it takes you back and affects productivity.*

That's why it's as important to value long-tenured employees as it is to appreciate the new blood. Equality plays a big role here as well. As a leader, you need to make a distinction between a new employee who is just starting up and an employee who has reached a certain level in the company after working hard and putting in those long hours for many years.

Though you need to be fair and treat everyone equally, you still do need to take into consideration an employee's seniority when it comes to pay, benefits, promotions and bonuses. I have seen and heard many leaders say that seniority shouldn't matter. Yes, if you're dealing with a weak link, I agree. But, when you have a hard working long-term employee and you are paying this person the same as someone who just started and has less experience, where's the incentive for the former to be loyal and commit to staying with an organization?

No one is perfect

It seems as if nowadays leaders enjoy showing off the power that comes with their position and their egos are inflated. Too often have I witnessed leaders who belittle their people in public for unnecessary and petty issues. I've heard leaders say, "No one is perfect," and, "Everyone needs to improve." I completely agree with both concepts. But, why would we not focus on a person's strong attributes? Why can't we support them to cultivate their qualities rather than focusing on what they can't do well and crush their spirit?

I have thought about this long and hard. My theory is that by giving employees reviews or feedback that tells them they need improvement or by pointing out the fact that they are not perfect, leaders feel in control of the situation, maintaining their power over their team. And, of course, when it's time for a raise or a promotion, these arguments can always be used as the reason a certain person wasn't considered for the promotion or didn't get the raise he or she thought they deserved.

The more I hear stories from various employees, it saddens me that, in today's corporate world, leaders seem to have lost touch with their inner True Self. They feel the need to pick on people and find something to fix about them, even if there is nothing that needs special attention.

If your team is working well, producing accurate and timely work, then do you really have to find something to fix just to boost your ego as the boss? Don't come up with a change just for the sake of change. Like the old saying goes, "Why fix something that's not broken?"

> *Don't come up with a change just for the sake of change.*

Don't get me wrong. I am not talking about trying to make improvements in the way we work, or the products we have to deliver. I'm referring to changes that don't add any value or do not improve results but just create unnecessary work. Time is of the essence. If you keep on adding activity on top of activity without putting much thought into the approach or the end result, you will not achieve much. Instead, you'll be taking away precious time from your team, reducing productivity, and, possibly even the level of service you provide your customers.

From the bottom up

If you look back at your humble beginnings and remember that you too had to start from the bottom, you will value and respect the folks sitting in their cubicles doing the dirty hard work, while you are enjoying your office with posh furniture and a beautiful view. It's important to connect with the front-line staff before making any procedural or administrative changes or even budget cuts, since the very same changes you think will be improvements may be the cause of turmoil for your employees.

Sadly, some leaders move up the ranks quickly either because they know someone who knows the hiring manager, or they are related to the owner of the company, or they look good on a résumé and have charisma. Because they have not worked in the trenches before moving up in their careers, these leaders don't always relate to or empathize with the daily work that must continue in order to keep a company going. If you are one of these leaders, stop barking out orders to people, disrespecting their feelings or the amount of work and time it would take to accomplish what you're asking for.

As I look back at all the years I spent doing the grunt work, I consider myself lucky to have started at the very bottom. As I have mentioned in the first pages of this book, more than 30 years ago, I started working as a telex and telephone operator. As the years went by, I moved up because of hard work, dedication and loyalty to each manager I worked for. Definitely, my beginning years have helped me set the foundation to appreciate what it means to do the daily work and the importance each employee brings to the company regardless of his or her position level.

POWER vs. *Heart* in Leadership

Closing Remarks

You can encourage a team, earn their trust, and continue to have their loyalty and respect, as long as you lead with your heart. That's *H -E -A -R -T*, heart. It doesn't take much to be a good leader so long as you are:

> *H*umble
>
> *E*galitarian
>
> *A*ppreciative
>
> *R*espectful, and
>
> *T*rustworthy

To recap, why are these five *human* attributes essential? Because if, along with that position power, you don't use the power of your *H -E -A -R -T,* even though you may be in a leadership role, with that fancy title, a huge office, and a team who seems to laugh at your jokes and jump each time you beckon, the minute you leave the room, your team will not hesitate to share their true feelings behind your back.

And, as soon as you lose that leadership role, no one will think you're funny any more! The people who were laughing at your jokes will actually be relieved and happy that you're no longer their leader. And, no one will even care what happens to you.

If you can master these five *human* attributes, you will always have a team that will follow you and support you to the best of their abilities, no matter what your leadership level. And, even if one day you lose your leadership position, or when a team member eventually decides to move up and take on different opportunities, I guarantee you that he or she will always continue to remember you with affection and respect. Not only that, but he or she will keep in touch with you and help you when you need support. You may even build strong lifelong friendships, so long as you are open to it. *I have.*

> *A true leader is one who is in touch with his or her True Self...*

A true leader is one who is in touch with her or his True Self and, at the same time, guides others to connect with their own true selves to help them lead fulfilled lives, not only at work but in their personal lives as well.

I want to leave you with one final thought...keep cultivating your *H -E -A -R -T* and use these five attributes everywhere you go. You and those around you will always benefit from them.

POWER vs. *Heart* in Leadership

About the Author

Ovsan brings a wealth of knowledge and global leadership experience, gained over 30-plus years. Her career started in Europe, then moved to Canada and now continues in the United States.

Over the years, Ovsan's genuine concern and sincere desire to help people has attracted colleagues and friends who have shared with her the difficulties and issues they have had with their own leaders and coworkers.

The implausible stories Ovsan has heard, bundled with her personal experiences, are the drive and passion behind her book "**POWER** vs. *Heart* in Leadership."

Ovsan is a speaker, a coach and a mentor to new managers and team members who are facing issues with their leaders or who want to move up in their careers. She speaks six languages and holds a master's degree in management and human resources management. Ovsan is also a certified brain management consultant.

For more information visit www.powervsheart.com.

POWER vs. *Heart* in Leadership

Made in the USA
San Bernardino, CA
08 October 2016